JANET OLEARSKI

was born in London and studied languages and linguistics at the University of Edinburgh, and later at the University of London Institute of Education. Her poetry, short fiction, and life writing have appeared in various publications including *Wasafiri*, *Litro*, *Bare Fiction*, *Far Off Places*, and *Big Wide Words (Poems on the Buses)*. She has authored several children's books, while for adults she has published two short-story collections, *A Brief History of Several Boyfriends* and *The Book of Reasonable Women*, and a novel, *A Traveller's Guide to Namisa*. She is a graduate of the Manchester Writing School at MMU and the founder of the Abu Dhabi Writers' Workshop. She has lived and worked in Italy, Poland, Oman, and the United Arab Emirates. She has lived in Central Portugal since 2018.

Read more at: www.janetolearski.com

AFTER THE FIRE

Poems

Janet Olearski

ISBN 978-989-53633-0-8 (Paperback)
ISBN 978-989-53633-1-5 (Ebook)

Cover Design: ebooklaunch.com
Cover Image: @janetolearski

*For my friend Annie Middlemiss, who saw it coming.
She was right. I should have followed her advice.*

Contents

The Fire Tree   1

Re-assembly Instructions   2

Burning Desire   5

A Reflected Woman   6

Advice   11

Sign of the Fox   12

A Cat Walks into a Bar   14

Snakes   15

Storage   16

Urban Nomad   18

Recognition   20

Exchange   21

Preparedness   23

Simplify   24

Aspiration   26

The Awakening   27

Gardening in Portugal   28

Alone Shark   29

Tractor Man   30

A Small Wish 31

Swimming Pool   32

Unassuming   33

A Brief Letter to My Father   34

Friends   35

Greener   36

Castle   37

In Memoriam   38

Wild Life   39

After Thought 41

Acknowledgements   43

***

The Fire Tree

After the fire, only one remains.
All that I find, I place under
this tree of lost things.
A small pink pencil to grow the child,
a key for the conservation of our world,
and looking ahead, a soiled and weathered
glove, pointing to the road we cannot see.
A watch, its beats crushed and stopped,
a blue plastic cable, curled like a snake,
tendrils exposed and disconnected.
In a tiny tub, tinted cream to magic away
the wrinkles in our plans,
a horseshoe embedded in the earth,
glinting from beneath the leaves.
A rope to skip or secure or pull,
a page of notes we should have read,
smudged by dew drops, a strip of foil,
its asprin blisters popped.
An empty beer bottle, its courage consumed,
And a piece of string, its length as yet unknown.
All tossed in the night wind, burned by the sun.
Will no one reclaim what is lost?

Re-assembly Instructions

For a newly purchased house,
devastated by Portuguese forest fires
in October 2017, here are your
re-assembly instructions.
But, read first the disclaimer...

since the materials are mainly
what you make of them, and take note
that steps 1 to 6 may well be more,
or fewer, than you could have imagined.
Check that you have items A to E.

A Arabian mau cats (x 4)
B Desert tortoises (x 4)
C Arabic-speaking parrot (x 1)
D Unemployed lecturer (x 1)
E Belongings (x far-too-many)

Step 1. Clear work space of burnt debris,
attach replacement windows,
ensure that the surfaces of bedroom (1),
bathroom (2), and kitchen (3) are clean before
applying unemployed lecturer (D).

Step 2. Nail down the support
of a kindly lawyer, and
of local municipality authorities.
Hammer home the urgency
of the reconstruction.

Step 3. Store belongings (E) until mostly forgotten.
Insert animals (A, B, C), and
secure with unconditional love.
Remove soot from paws and claws.
Brush away own tears of uncertainty.

Step 4. Excavate hole within sight of house, and
dispose of any animal (A, B, or C)
that simply doesn't make it.
Install marker in memory to
remember them always.

Step 5. Fix whatever is possible
with hope and the patience of despair.
Draw close animals that remain
(A, and/or B, and/or C), and
fit tightly in place, as originally intended.

Step 6. Screw all those who said
you shouldn't have bought a house
in a forest in Portugal in the first place.
Pull everything together, bending if necessary,
so as to prove them completely wrong.

Burning Desire

For years she searched to find her special home.
She looked in Ireland, Italy, Poland.
Discovered it hiding, incognito,
in the eucalyptus-breathing forests
of Portugal. And there she found herself
in love with its woody porch, its flowers,
its vines entwined and secured for safety,
far away from the evil of the eye.
So, with her desires, she enveloped it,
as did wild fires. Entitled, possessive.

A Reflected Woman

Reflection One.

Eyes, blue like my mother's,
worried like my father's.

Hair, freshly strimmed,
the texture of dry grass,
the colour of blanched cedar.

Skin, nibbled by sun
and ancient acne,
a mottled tan like
an unfavourite pair of shoes
from school.

Failed cheeks, dabbed pink,
their downward descent
already begun into the face's
newly revealed valleys.

Mouth wordless, faded,
nothing more to say.

Eyebrows thin, almost transparent,
arching in surprise or,
more likely, disappointment.

Tiny pinpricks in ear lobes,
though no light or sound
shine through.

Around my throat,
a single gold chain,
once a lover's snare.

Then, dulled and ashen, a cardigan,
anonymous, unzipped, enhanced
by a matching grey cat,
soft haired but tarnished
by too long a journey,
one white paw stretched and
clinging to the links at my neck,
the other wrapping itself
in need and trust
around my upper arm.

Its eyes, glazed and sickly,
watch me through the mirror,
its tail waving and flapping

across the fabric of my guilt,
its mucus-filled nose
nudging against mine as,
uprooted, optionless,
both waiting, we exchange
our still living breaths.

Reflection Two.

Here is post-apocalyptic living,
setting a trend in shades of pitch.

But see how hard
I have tried to scrub loose
the black grime
engrained in floor tiles,
have tried to sweep, to wash away
the leaden dust that wafts down
from walls and ceilings,
have tried to wipe clean
door handles, furniture, shelves,
yet still the filth sticks,
comes back, still resists,
as though the house takes pride
in its carbonized persona.

Now look closely.

You'll see the window sills
rubber-stamped with paw prints.

You'll see spiders' webs in corners,
draped across skirting boards,
hanging like discarded shreds
of black lace.

On the smoke-stained walls,
perhaps you'll see, as I do,
images of winged horses,
of blizzard-blown buildings,
of sea monsters, or prehistoric animals,
rising through the splattered plaster.

Then, inside my cupboards,
you'll see where the oily smoke,
burnt out, came to rest.

You'll see down a corridor
to where light fittings
hang like plastic stalactites,
you'll see a jigsaw puzzle of cracks
in the glass panels of my front door

and, behind me, cluttered,
you'll see the kitchen table,
its collection of useless medicines
for a self-cancelling cat.

Reflection Three.

What you cannot see from here
are the night-time tears,
this business of grieving
for so much that is lost,
or about to be.

Advice

Don't mention the fire.
People will go silent,
not knowing what to say.

They may seem sorry,
or sad, or just glad
it didn't happen to them.

They may think you are jinxed,
that the jinxiness will rub off,
bringing them misfortune.

They may think it best
to stay away, not to touch,
not to get involved.

They'll need a moment to fix their faces,
eyes lowered, mournful looks.
This would be correct.

But, conceal the soot, the stains,
the ashen thoughts, and
say simply, 'Fire. What fire?'

Sign of the Fox

This morning I saw
a fox. A cat, I
thought, but hefty for
a cat. A dog, I
thought, but its tail was
bushy for a dog's.
Then I saw its snout,
longish and pointed.
Yes, a fox for sure.

This morning I saw
a fox, and it saw
me, I thought. Waiting,
since there was something
for me to be told.
Sooner he could have
flown, and not waited
there, exposed, for me
to spot him purposeful.

This morning I saw
a fox, safeguarding
a private message,
that I am anxious
to receive soonest,
to be revealed to
me in due course, though
if I thought at length,
I would know, foxless.

A Cat Walks into a Bar

A cat walks into a bar.

She is nocturnal.
She speaks a language
I only half understand.
She is mean, selfish, vengeful.
We are alike.
A cause for concern,

this absence.
She has been with me
for so many years.
My love,
unconditional,
and now it's over,

the cleaning
of the litter tray,
the mopping up of barf,
the purchase of costly foods
for a fussy eater.
Liberated.

And doesn't come back out.

Snakes

The occasional snake
scrolls out from the undergrowth.

I could delete it, but
I am too kind for that.

I ignore it, leave it
to slide away shameful.

The unimportant must learn
to remove themselves.

Storage

Boxes. Building blocks.
Like the tree houses
that as children we
played in. Damp cardboard
boxes in which the
cat sleeps, enjoying
the comfort of space,
enclosed, dark, warm, but
here taped shut, stacked, blocks
of lead too heavy
to lift, now barring
passage, preventing
the seeing of chinked
light, solid like the
paving stones outside,
soot-coated from the
fire, where we leave our
footprints in the rain,
our weight imprinting
a passing sign of
us, the heaviness

of ourselves, of all
possessed the volume,
encapsulated
in these containers,
fragments of our lives.

Urban Nomad

I was born of the city, its streets, sloping roofs,
its bricks, buses, cars, traffic lights, sirens,
the hooves on tarmac of early morning cavalry,
trees at my window four storeys above,
resolved to reach a purer air,
dragging imprisoned roots through paving stones.
And, on the slates and on the abandoned chimneys,
escapee peacocks, misfortune-free, strut and echo
    citywise.

Then other places, rooms within rooms, doors within
    doors,
opening to domes, bell towers, roof gardens,
washing lines on wrought iron balconies, a distant
    mountain,
the absorbent backcloth of a ship in the port,
made hazy by a sizzling sun. Or elsewhere, to the north,
a silent city in winter, once grey, landscaped white,
soft with layers of fallen flakes,
pavements perilous underfoot, leaveless.

Later still, escape to light, persistent and obsessive,
to the six-lane highways, burning sands,
palm fronds swaying, crackling, rustling,
when the stifled air is unstilled
and the desert floats its grains under doors
and through the narrowest of window slits,
dusting the frangipane, resilient, tricklefed.

And the transformation, the search, almost complete,
through age, a need for a less that is more,
the city nearly gone, roads now fields,
roofs now treetops, misted lines
of land and forest for horizons, and somewhere,
merged with the night-time howls of dogs,
the strutting and calling of peacocks.

Recognition

You are all alone.
No one expected.
No one will see you.
So, why the make-up?

When I look in the
mirror, I want to
recognize something
of my former self.

I want to be sure
that she is still there.

Exchange

'*Ya habibti*, how do you like it here?'
This they ask me, but reject my answer.
'No,' they say, 'that is wrong, for you must say…'

I must say, like it or not – I do not,
'*al-hamdulillah*.'

I am ambiguous in my dislike
of the heat, the dust, the humidity,
colourlessness, and uniformity.

Watching the palm fronds wave at my windows,
I recall multicoloured green, damp grass,
the voices of the rain, desiring these
over so many years until they say,

'*Habibti, khallas. Ma'a as-salama.*
Your wise old blood is no longer needed.
You can return now to that other place.'

In grains of remembered sand, I would count
time, but they are too many and too fine.
'How do you like it here?' they ask. I say,
'*al-hamdulillah*.'

'No,' they say. 'That is wrong. You are misplaced,
You are mistaken, forgetting yourself.
For you must say instead, *Está bom aqui.'*

I will, if you say so, though it is not,
since I recall heat, humidity, dust,
all of it missing, the colourlessness,
blotted by green. Heavy under the rain.

Preparedness

If she had not prepared for the storm,
the consequences would have been disastrous.
Deckchairs blown into nearby fields,
tiles swept from the porch roof,
garden furniture splintered into
pieces of wood ready for the next bonfire,
plant pots smashed, flowers butchered,
her life disrupted, a loss of order.

She did prepare for the storm.
Deckchairs folded, tiles secured,
garden furniture shifted and stacked,
pots and flowers in places of safety.

But since the storm never came,
she moved everything back though,
for the life of her, where it all originally went
she could scarce remember.

Simplify

Today I simply want to do nothing.
Today, as the wind hurls itself against the trees and
propels itself through waves of grass,
I simply want to do *nada*.

My best plans from yesterday have gone astray.
I have helped them out of the door.
I am not obliged to follow the rules
of the person I was before.

Today there is a staccato sun, a thickening heat
and, if I keep my head down,
I can catch the underlying tranquility
of that moment so often lost to commitment.

And beneath the tumult of this argumentative gale,
there is really only stillness. There is a smartphone,
but not now. There is a to-do list that can be done later.
There is responsibility, but not now.

Who will grumble that I am not gainfully employed?
I might have been, but I've decided that I won't.
Who will read posts about goal-setting,
or about procrastination, and feel guilt?

Guilty are those who never tried
sitting without purpose under the storm.

Aspiration

A poet tries
to learn a
language, even
Portuguese,
but it will be
a long time
before she gets
to follow
in the path of
Camões,
or Florbela,
or Verde,
or Pessoa.
If ever.

The Awakening

The poet wakes in the morning
to the mewing of her cat
and fur in her nostrils.
The view from her window,
the poet's, not the cat's,
is as it was
the day before,
the distant forest
perhaps a little lighter,
perhaps a little darker.
And she can hear the sea,
or, was that the cat,
thinking of his tuna
and seafood selections?

Gardening in Portugal

Must I document
my decline?
'Hello, how are you?'
'Not well,' I say.

The healthiness
I imagined for myself
was indeed imaginary,
for I never bloomed
after replanting.

Alone Shark

You'll need to be gregarious,
an extrovert, but also,
apparently, quite helpless.

You'll need to be monied,
to put your hand in your pocket,
to pay without flinching.

You'll need to be demanding,
bossy, compelling, to seek
without shame first place in the queue.

You'll need to let me know
how it's done, how you get on,
how to be you and learn from your example.

Tractor Man

Put away the machete.
Now we can see the view.
Tractor Man, tracked down
at last, came and made new.

Trundling fore and aft,
crushing and cutting all underfoot,
the high brown grasses gone
in the sweaty heat of an afternoon.

Hear the dismay of birds,
rising from crisp shrubbery.
See the fragmented solar lights.
Weep for the broken roses.

The fires are to be disappointed
by lack of fodder for their flames,
a commitment fulfilled, a burden
lifted from an accidental landowner.

A job well done by Tractor Man,
a bargain at sixty euros, and
an icy bottle of local beer,
wrenched open with his teeth.

A Small Wish

And this always,
to wake up
happy and see
the land breathe.

Swimming Pool

What will I remember you for?
Probably for your swimming pool,
which overfilled itself on my watch.

Yet, chastened, I confessed my guilt
of not paying enough attention
to that or, more importantly, much later,

of any chance I might have had
of finding you again, even though
you once lived so close to my heart.

Unassuming

I assumed I would always be mobile,
that my hair would remain thick and weighty,
without brittle glints of scalp showing through,
no widening, like the seas, of my parting.
I assumed I would always hear a pin
eavesdrop, that my skin would be smooth and tan,
eyes not, like my mother's, bagged and drooping,
disappointed to see in shop windows
a familiar reflection of some old
person, less straight, hunched, slow, so imperfect.

A Brief Letter to My Father
24 September, 2021

Father, there are some things I'd like to tell you.

It is 2016. A Black American is President.
I've had some poems published.
I have four cats, two parrots, and eight tortoises.
I live in the UAE. It's hot here.

Father, there are some more things, I'd like to tell you.

It is 2021. I own my own house and everything in it.
We are hiding from something called Covid.
I am old. I have one cat, one parrot, and three tortoises.
I live in Portugal. It is hot here when it is not raining.

Father, in both cases, you are dead.

Friends

Over time I learned to distinguish
friend from acquaintance.

You are not my friend
if I pay for your services.

I learned to self-drive, self-manage,
self-motivate, even to cook for one.

I made friends with the land,
flowers, the fruit, the animals.

I made friends with a healing house.
No tears for a lack of friends.

Greener

How disappointed you are with the fruits of the soil.
The seeds you planted never flowered as imagined.
You are angry and resentful, sowing only blame.
For, as you know, it was not meant to be like this.

Our patch of earth has become ugly and chaotic.
You wanted it tamed and pliant, desiring perfection,
denying that it might have a will of its own, and
running with its rebelliousness, until it became unruly.

Yet, you did nothing to nourish it,
and now you disown it, want no part of it.
You have fallen out of love with the land that grew you.

So, drop tools and wander until you find
the place where you were meant to be.
We did it, some of us, still searching the greener grass.

Castle

Today will be a rainy day,
or worse.
There are storm clouds
on my App.
The trees tremble,
as if telepathic.
Flowers sway, lean forward
in anticipation.
A cat sits in wait, humid,
on the kitchen window ledge.
Strutting by, a cockerel
shouts warnings.
My house is a castle,
a fortress, drawbridge up,
blinds down, curtains closed.

I am protected from bad weather,
from a tempestuous world.

In Memoriam

Who can capture it,
your absence from the world?
That footfall, remembered,
but no longer felt,

heard in memory alone.
That breeze, its touch invisible,
fingers of air
through strands of hair.

That sight of sky, turning to blue
as the day opens.
Postcards of landscape
never again seen.

The shadow in a patch of sunlight
that you have become.

Wild Life

A bird died this morning. Wind-thrown
from nowhere against my window pane,
I could do nothing to save her.

Crashed to the floor of my porch, startled
to find herself where she had never intended to be,
her bird-expression as if surprised

to be on the ground, to be alive, to be saved,
to not be herself, to see the approach of death.
Then, from impact to hand, life-drained.

I would wait forever for her to revive,
to return from wherever dead birds go,
body, feathers, her softening eye, faultless.

I tread through brambles, stumble over stones.
Thorns catch, gripping me as I pass,
wanting to know what I hold.

Searching, I see no last place for her to rest
with dignity, with honour, in a celebration of
her once-freedom, her wild life of air and clouds.

Except perhaps under a rosebush in bloom,
where, perfect and whole, she may wait
on moist soil, familiar earth, for time to take her.

So will we all one day be surprised by death,
in a blast of air, in a spin of breath,
returning, cupped in the hands of God.

After Thought

Long after the fire
comes the after-thought,
which was that
she had prayed for
a life-changing experience.
After which, her house
burned down, thus
enabling her to understand
the power of prayer and
causing her to vow
never to ask again.

Acknowledgements

'A Reflected Woman' was longlisted for the *Bridport Poetry Prize 2020*; 'Lost,' a shortened version of 'The Fire Tree' was published in *In the voice of trees* (Cinnamon Press: 2020); 'The Awakening' appeared in *Far Off Places*; 'Exchange' was longlisted for the *AUB International Poetry Prize 2021* and the *Aurora Prize for Poetry 2021*.

After The Fire was shortlisted for the Cinnamon Pamphlet Award 2022

*

My special thanks go to Cristiana Silva Ferreira, Ros and David Greenway, Albertino Santos, Filipe Abrantes, Alcino Filipe Francisco, the Municipality of Penacova, and to all those who made possible the renovation of my house in Lagares, Travanca do Mondego, Portugal, following the forest fires of October 2017.

***

THE BOOK OF REASONABLE WOMEN

Stories

Janet Olearski

The women in these stories are at all times, through their many varied emotions, entirely reasonable... at least to themselves. They each do what they need to do and believe what they need to believe. They are trustful, loyal, and believing, but also heedless, rash, and detached. They fall in and out of love, they suffer and overcome loss and, when things go wrong, they simply start again. Their experiences make them resilient, unfazed, practical, but also demanding, persistent, determined. Would they lie to you, conjure up ghosts, steal your lover, put a spell on you? Probably. Yes.

The Book of Reasonable Women is a collection of thirty contemporary short stories, exploring themes of assimilation, identity, ethnicity, accountability, self-reliance, remembering, and entirely purposeful forgetting. It illustrates both with humour and compassion the remarkable reasonableness of women.

ISBN: 978-989-53381-8-4

A BRIEF HISTORY OF SEVERAL BOYFRIENDS

Stories

Janet Olearski

They are almost boyfriends, disgraced boyfriends, never-going-to-happen boyfriends, live-in boyfriends, dishonest boyfriends, obsessive boyfriends, dead boyfriends. Their history is brief because they didn't make the grade or, unfortunately for them, they just didn't survive.

Twenty-five thought-provoking, table-turning stories in which women stray knowingly into relationships that they may regret. And deal with them.

ISBN: 978-989-53381-4-6

A TRAVELLER'S GUIDE TO NAMISA

a novel

Janet Olearski

Philip Blair, an innocent posted abroad, must form his own judgement of Namisa, a conservative country rich in tradition, ready to embrace new beliefs on the back-cloth of the Namisan *autumn-autumn* and the Pundexit Crisis. But, will having a fake marriage with Felicity, an on-the-rebound romance novelist, compromise his principles and prevent him from finding true love?

A Traveller's Guide to Namisa is an enthralling story of intercultural miscommunication, corruption, depravity, multicoloured cocktails, and PhDs.

ISBN: 978-989-53381-2-2

9 789898 536330 8